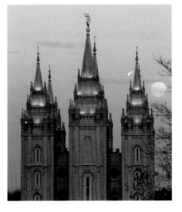

TEMPLE SQUARE

IN THE LIGHT OF ITS SEASONS

DON BUSATH

EAGLE GATE

SALT LAKE CITY, UTAH

Visit us at www.deseretbook.com

Library of Congress Cataloging-in-Publication Data
Busath, Don.
    Temple Square : in the light of its seasons / Don Busath.
      p.   cm.
ISBN 1-57345-847-3
      1. Temple Square (Salt Lake City, Utah)—Pictorial works.   2. Salt Lake City (Utah)—Buildings, structures, etc.—Pictorial works.   I. Title.

    F834.S27 T463   2001
    979.2'258—dc21
                                                    2001001482

Printed in Hong Kong through Palace Press International   68875-6739

10   9   8   7   6   5   4   3   2

INTRODUCTION

MOST RESIDENTS of Salt Lake City accept the Salt Lake Temple as the focal point of the city's downtown. To the city, it is the literal hub from which streets receive their names: South Temple, North Temple, Second South (the second street south of the temple), Fifth East, and so on. To faithful members of The Church of Jesus Christ of Latter-day Saints, it is the "mother" temple of the Church and is a sacred and holy place.

The temple, however, is just one of the buildings—some new, some historical—found on the temple block. The block's other buildings include the Church's international headquarters, the Family History Library, the Joseph Smith Memorial Building, and the Beehive House—office and home to early Church president Brigham Young. Surrounding these buildings, which serve members of The Church of Jesus Christ of Latter-day Saints and others affected by its work, are beautiful gardens, walkways, pools, and sculptures that enhance and beautify. The block, in turn, is surrounded by malls, office buildings, and hotels.

Many visitors to Temple Square experience special feelings while there. I have that reaction myself, even though I have come to the complex often during my sixty-eight years. Besides enjoying the gardens and taking photographs, I come to worship, enjoy concerts, and attend special functions, such as temple marriages and temple work. I hope this visual tribute captures some of the calm reverential feelings I experience whenever I enter the temple grounds.

ABOUT THE COVER

I WAS AWED BY THE HUGE, nearly full moon hanging low over the horizon as I crested the hill on First Avenue in downtown Salt Lake City. I was on my way to a 6 A.M. appointment and was momentarily irritated, as I usually am when I see a breathtaking scene but have 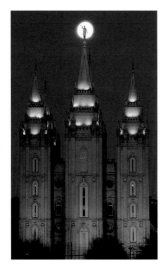 no camera and no time to capture it. Then it dawned on me that if the weather remained good the following morning, I could see the full moon set right over the Salt Lake Temple.

The next morning I was up early to check. No clouds! I gathered my long lenses and heavy tripod and hurried west on First Avenue. As the temple spires came into sight, the big full moon was hanging directly over the center spire, atop which stood a statue of the angel Moroni. The skylight was perfectly balanced—strong enough to separate the spires but weak enough to allow the moon to still shine brightly. The combination of the setting moon, skylight, weather, and spires provided me with a once-in-a-lifetime opportunity. I parked, fumbled my camera onto the tripod as fast as I could, and set up in the middle of the street.

The moon moved so fast, however, that by the time I aligned the telephoto lens, focused, and shot, the angel Moroni was at the edge of the circumference of the setting moon. Several times I hurriedly backpedaled up the hill, set up, and shot again—all the while dodging traffic and insults from angry motorists. By the time I finished shooting, the sky was light, the moon was out of range and to one side of the statue, and I was a block away from where I had started.

I realized later that this experience reaffirmed my belief that our time on earth is brief and therefore precious. The moon that seems to hang in the sky actually moves quickly in its orbit around the earth; the earth, in turn, spins with unrelenting steadiness on its axis. The days and nights turn quickly into years, and the years into a lifetime. In the interim, little things prove to be important, and small periods of time turn into defining moments.

Right: The temple rises from a verdant carpet of lush spring foliage highlighted by accents of color.

Above: Surrounding buildings loom higher, but the Salt Lake Temple and its six unique spires capture the attention and nourish the eye, drawing it heavenward.

Right: Soft light on the Conference Center gives a quiet dignity and feeling of holiness to the architecture.

Above: The reflection pool smiles a friendly welcome, reflecting the plaza that has replaced a block of Main Street.

Right: The Church Office Building of The Church of Jesus Christ of Latter-day Saints rises twenty-eight stories above the plaza.

Above: The sun breaks the horizon,
casting a sublime light on Temple Square.

Right: Bright pansies and tulips announce spring's coming
throughout Temple Square. The temple and plaza grounds owe their
beauty to landscape architects and the fastidious planning and
careful work of master gardeners, who replant the grounds as the
seasons change. Color and texture are optimal throughout the summer.

Following page: This grand view of the Conference Center, Salt Lake
Temple, and surrounding city buildings exhibits the warmth and
welcome so typical in the evenings as folks come to enjoy concerts and
activities in this part of downtown.

This area near the Assembly Hall gives
the effect of a quiet country garden. New
visitors are often surprised by the beauty
of Temple Square and the contrast it offers
to the hustle and bustle of nearby streets.

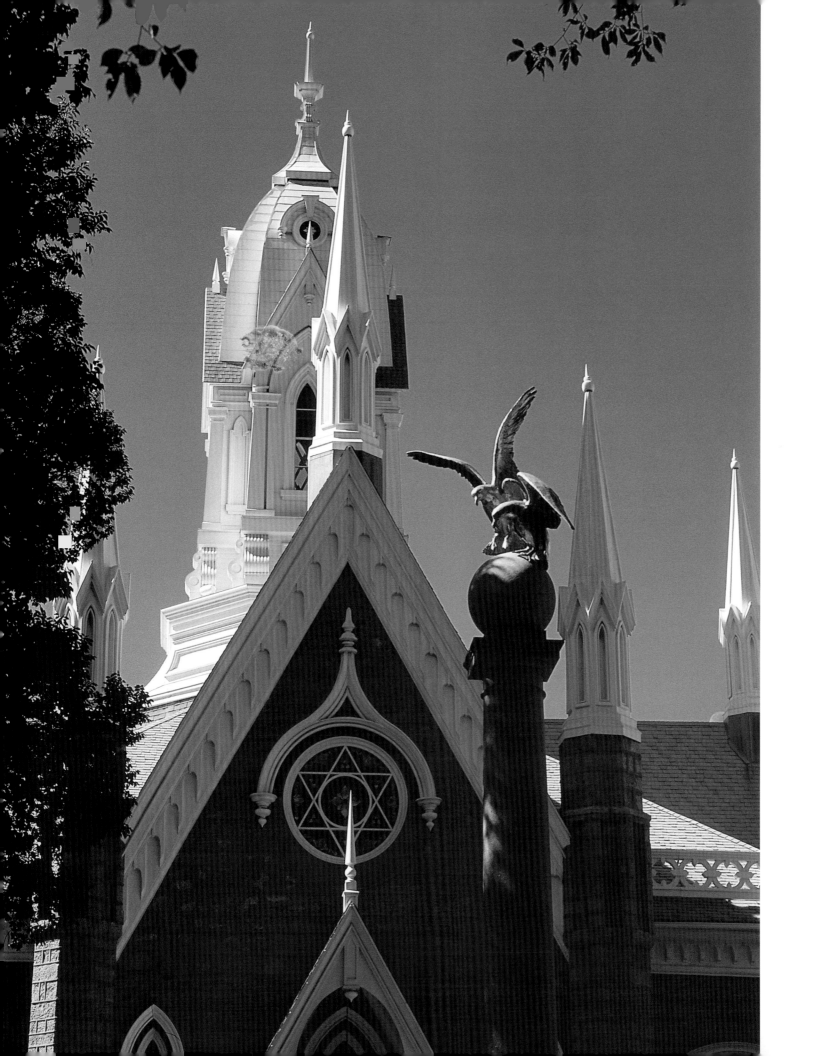

Left: In 1913, Mahonri Young sculpted the seagulls and designed the monument depicting the "Miracle of the Gulls" that saved the crops of the early pioneers from an invasion of crickets. He also designed and produced the This Is the Place Monument east of the city.

Right: The statues of Joseph Smith and Hyrum Smith, sculpted by Mahonri Young, stand south of the temple. The brothers, who loved each other deeply, died together as martyrs for their faith.

Above: A latticework of new spring blossoms and dark winter limbs proclaims a new season outside the Assembly Hall.

Right: In the dusk-rose of evening, Aldo Rebechi's replica of The Christus, *by famed Danish sculptor Bertel Thorvaldsen, invites visitors to the North Visitors' Center.*

Above: The sculptural grouping Joyful
Moment *seems right at home in this setting on
the plaza. Sculptor Dennis Smith is well
known for his contemporary sculptures of
women and children.*

*Right: Cherry tree blossoms burst forth with
the promise of new life—a promise central to
the work performed inside the temple.*

Left: The Nauvoo bell, part of the Relief Society Centennial Memorial, originally hung in the Nauvoo Temple.

Right: The red crescent moon above the cool lights of the temple spires creates an unusual feeling of contrast.

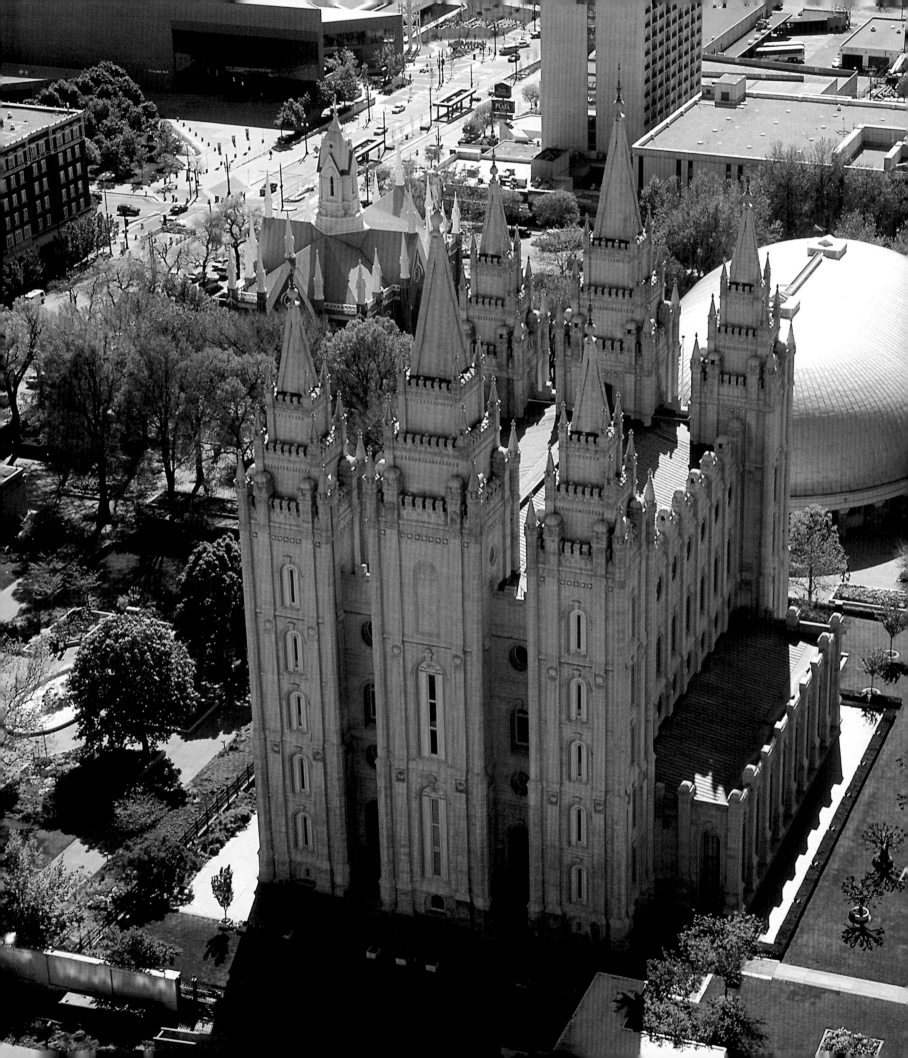

Above: Italian sculptor Aldo Rebechi produced this marble replica of Thorvaldsen's Christus, housed in the rotunda of the North Visitors' Center.

Left: The observation deck of the Church Office Building offers this bird's-eye view of the order and symmetry of the temple block, found within walking distance of the Salt Palace Convention Center, the Maurice Abravanel (Symphony) Hall, and the Delta Center.

Left: The temple's silhouetted spires seem to offer an anchor against the wind and rain of a gathering storm.

Right: A doorknob on one of the temple's massive east- and west-side doors shows the building's forty-year construction period: 1853–1893. These four doors are not currently used as entrances to the temple.

*This wonderful depiction of a handcart family
has become an icon for many LDS faithful
whose ancestors used this form of transportation
to cross the plains. The heroic-sized bronze
grouping, originally created on a smaller scale
in 1926 by Norwegian sculptor Torlief
Knaphus, has a look of realism and
determination.*

Reminiscent of the past, the horse and carriage
provide a pleasant way to tour downtown
Salt Lake City today.

Above: The temple stone is sculpted with symbols and details that have meaning and interest for those with a knowledge of the roles temples played throughout antiquity.

Right: Lavender spires and a sinking moon indicate life and movement in a restful scene.

The Tabernacle, home to the Mormon Tabernacle Choir, is
a truly unusual and unique building in which form
following function makes for a useful, practical meeting
hall that has served the community and The Church of
Jesus Christ of Latter-day Saints since the building was
completed in 1867. During the early years of the Church,
the hall served as the main meeting place in the valley.
Sessions of the Church's semiannual general conference were
held in the Tabernacle until October 1999. Until the
nearby Maurice Abravanel Hall was completed in 1979,
the Tabernacle was also home to the Utah Symphony.

The Tabernacle features distinctive acoustics. A pin
dropped at the front of the hall can be heard without
amplification at the very back of the hall. Even when its
benches are filled, the Tabernacle has an intimate and
homey pioneer feeling.

Above: Bright-colored leaves mark the
changing of the seasons on Temple Square.

Right: The craftsmanship of the pioneers is
evident in this rounded corner of the
Tabernacle's domed roof, which curves under
the stately gaze of the temple.

Above: Sunset-charged clouds draw a red blanket over Temple Square as the day bids a dramatic adieu to Salt Lake City.

Left: The Conference Center stands like a majestic sentinel in the evening light.

Above: The quiet obscurity that at times blankets the Salt Lake Valley complements the gray-white tones of the granite stones.

Right: The winter season presents a special splendor in the abstractions of form. The eye for lovely design often fails when the body is rigid with cold, but the seeker finds reward in looking beyond discomfort.

*The large windows of
the North Visitors'
Center frame the
brutal beauty of
blizzard conditions on
Temple Square.*

Two sister missionaries brave the elements to greet visitors with smiles and information. Sister missionaries assigned to Temple Square hail from all over the world.

*The Assembly Hall and temple
seem frozen in a long winter.
Fortunately, temperatures in the
Salt Lake Valley change often and
abruptly, frequently altering the
valley's frigid beauty.*

*Lights and concerts draw thousands
to Temple Square throughout the
holiday season, from Thanksgiving
to New Year's Day.*

Members of the Mormon
Tabernacle Choir pose in a
Christmas setting in the
Tabernacle.

A fairyland of Christmas lights thrills
young children and most adults as well.
Preparation for this spectacular display
begins in early fall.

Above: The Tabernacle and the Christmas lights frame the Utah Capitol Building as carolers share the music of Christmas.

Right: Snow-covered tree limbs provide a natural frame for the statue of the angel Moroni.

Above: Lights dramatize the Assembly Hall at dusk.

Right: The lighted temple stands as a fortress against the approaching nightfall.

*Above: Rising above the Temple
Square wall, these reflected dusk
views intrigue the camera eye.*

*Left: The spires of the venerable
Assembly Hall have a charm and
pleasing grace.*

Left: Salt Lake City streets were named and numbered from this site. Brigham Young designated the temple site, and Orson Pratt and Henry G. Sherwood fixed this spot as the meridian on 3 August 1847. David H. Burr, first U.S. surveyor-general for Utah, set the stone monument in 1855.

Right: This monument honoring Brigham Young and the pioneers, unveiled 24 July 1897, stands at the head of Main Street. Brigham Young directed that the Salt Lake Temple be constructed to stand into the Millennium.

*Above: Evening falls on the
Relief Society Building, which
was dedicated in 1956.*

*Left: This fish-eye view of the
Temple Square plaza illustrates
a symmetry of belonging.*

*The plaza offers a peaceful place
to walk and meditate during fall's
warm afternoons.*

*The plaza's reflection pool captures the
Relief Society Building on a bright
summer day.*

The lovely gold of the ranunculus is repeated in the warmth of the early light on the temple and the Church Office Building, with its bas-relief world map.

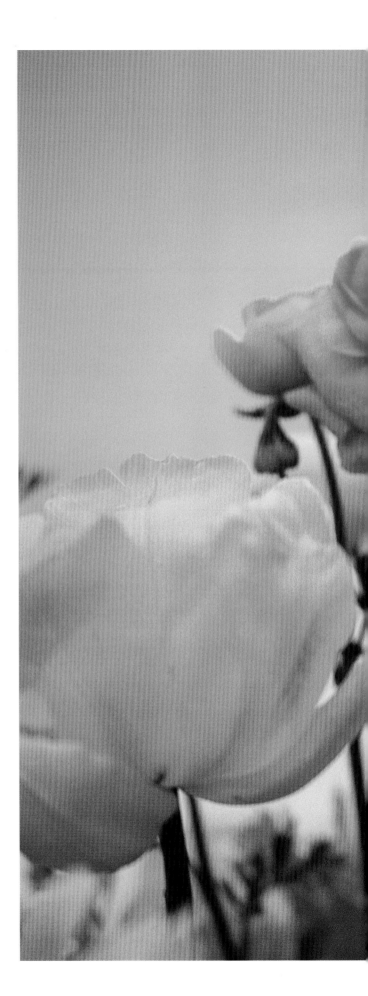

*Flowers and the plaza fountain
south of the Church Office Building
reach heavenward.*

Above: When the leaves are sparse on the trees of First Avenue, the spires of the temple seem to rise from the street. The sight of the sun setting in line with the confluence of street and spires is even more uncommon.

Left: City Creek Park makes an attractive foreground for the Church Office Building and temple.

Above: The Eagle Gate eagle flies amid a lofty glass and metal environment.

Right: Eagle Gate, a well-recognized landmark, embraces the historic Beehive House and the modern Church Office Building. The gate signifies the conclusion of the broad street that served as a major artery to bring the south valley population downtown. Laid out by Brigham Young to be straight and true, State Street linked many small communities from the north and south ends of the valley. To the north, Eagle Gate frames the dome of the Utah Capitol. A smaller version of the gate originally marked the entrance to Brigham Young's property and farm.

These scenes offer vignettes of the Lion House (left) and Beehive House (right), original home and property of Brigham Young, who led the Latter-day Saints westward and established a city in the desert wilderness. Brigham Young, who directed his people from here, felt that the cultural elements of life were important to the pioneer Saints. These houses, maintained and furnished as they would have been in his day, set standards worth emulating.

*Above: 47 East South Temple is an
address of great significance to
members and leaders of The Church
of Jesus Christ of Latter-day
Saints. With great anticipation,
many Latter-day Saints have
walked up the steps of the Church
Administration Building since its
completion in 1914.*

*Right: The austere columns of
the Church Administration
Building contrast with the
cheerful color of the adjacent
flower gardens.*

Above: The commercial neighborhood near the temple complex includes two busy shopping malls, hotels, the Salt Palace Convention Center, Salt Lake Art Center, and Maurice Abravanel Hall.

Right: A spring rain adds to the plaza's elegance.

Above: The firm that built the Joseph Smith Memorial Building (formerly the Hotel Utah) called the structure "the most perfectly arranged Hotel in the United States." Completed in 1911 in an Italian Renaissance style, the building features an exterior face of gleaming-white glazed brick and terra-cotta. During the building's hotel days, guests included every president of the United States between 1911 and 1992, when the hotel became the Joseph Smith Memorial Building. In addition, the hotel hosted numerous gubernatorial balls, lavish receptions and dinners, and many civic and social gatherings. The remodeled building retains all the grandeur and warmth of the old hotel.

Right: The impressive lobby of the Joseph Smith Memorial Building features a large marble figure of the Prophet Joseph Smith. The statue is an enlarged replica of an original bronze sculpture by Mahonri Young, found on Temple Square between the temple and the South Visitors' Center.

*Above: A lovely bed of tulips frames a
row of terra-cotta lion heads along the
north façade of the Joseph Smith
Memorial Building.*

*Right: Ceiling lights cast their warm glow
throughout the lobby of the Joseph Smith
Memorial Building. Two popular
restaurants operate on the building's top
floor, and subtle changes and upgrades
allow the former hotel to continue hosting
receptions and social functions. The Joseph
Smith Memorial Building houses Church
offices, a Church materials distribution
center, and a chapel for worship services.
In addition, it is home to the Legacy
Theater and a family history center, both
open to the public.*

*Above: This panoramic scene of South Temple Street
shows, left to right, the Church Administration Building,
Lion House, office of Brigham Young, Church Office
Building (behind), Beehive House, Utah Capitol dome,
and Eagle Gate.*

*Right: The glass surface of nearby Maurice Abravanel
Hall reflects the temple block.*

*Genealogists and others interested in family history come
from near and far to use the LDS Family History Library,
considered to be the most complete of its kind in the world.*

*The Museum of Church History and Art, located just west
of Temple Square, tells the story of The Church of Jesus
Christ of Latter-day Saints through programs and exhibits.*

Left: Granite steps lead toward the inviting beauty of the Conference Center.

Above: The entry hall of the Conference Center, featuring the family sculpture New Frontiers, by Avard Fairbanks, shows the expanse and grandeur of the center's interior.

Above: The Conference Center's Hall of the Prophets features sculpted busts of all fifteen men who have led The Church of Jesus Christ of Latter-day Saints.

Right: The Conference Center's 21,000-seat auditorium fills to capacity during general conference.

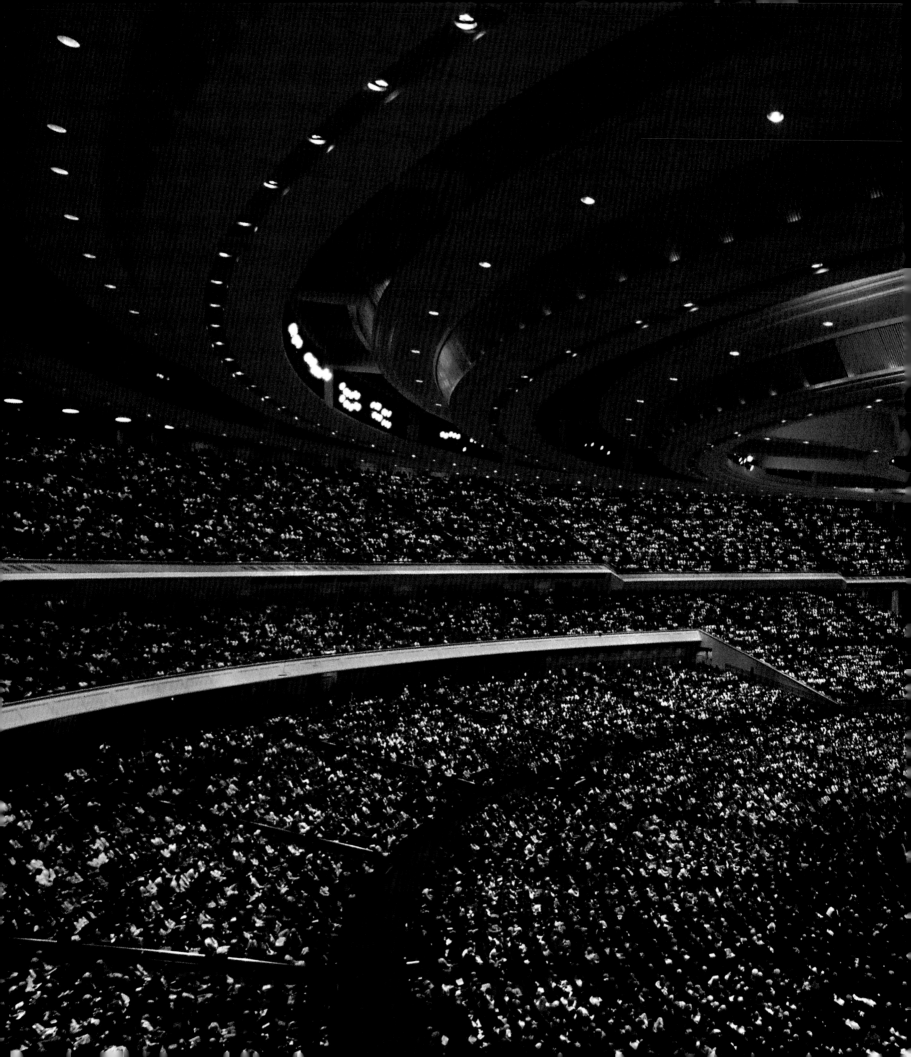

*Above: Trees, gardens, waterways,
and a fountain adorn the roof of the
Conference Center.*

*Left: Church members gather in the
Conference Center for the building's
dedication in October 2000.*

Above: The lighted Conference Center adds a stately, calm presence to downtown Salt Lake City.

Right: Latter-day Saints converge on the Conference Center for general conference.

Following page: As night settles over downtown Salt Lake City, the Salt Lake Temple remains a lighted beacon.

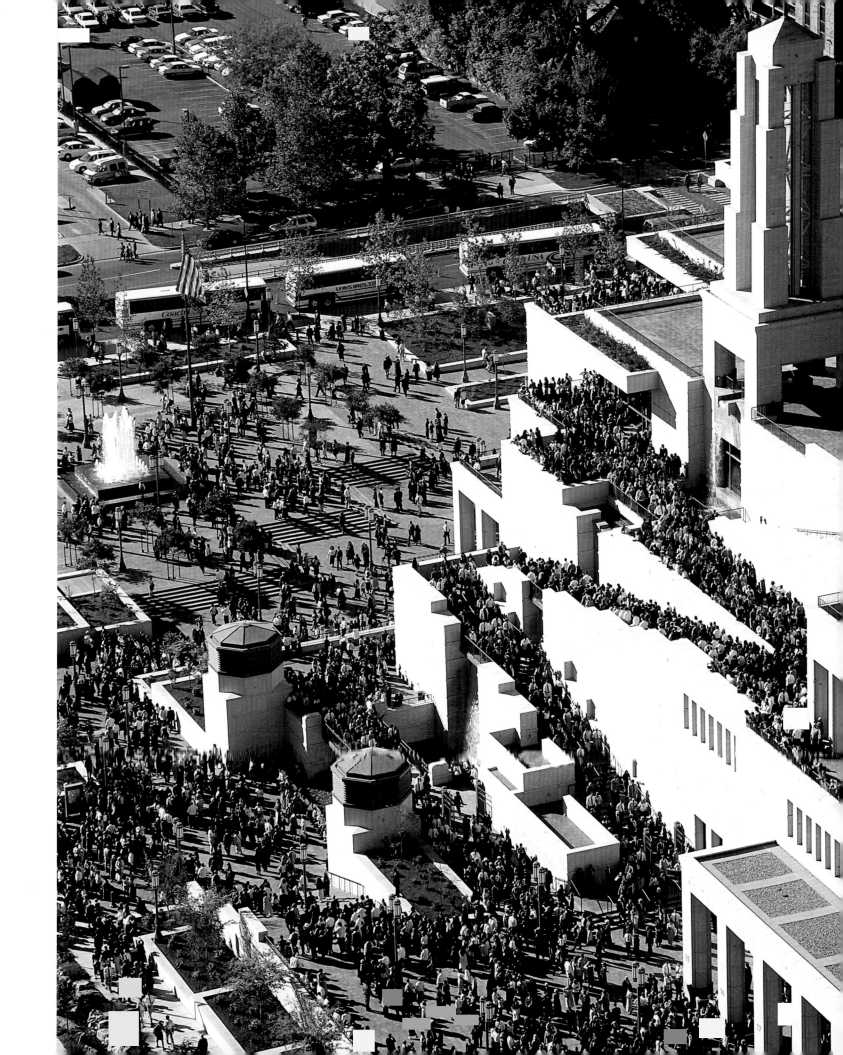

The Assembly Hall, whose spires sit atop what were once chimneys, was built of granite stone left over from the construction of the Salt Lake Temple.

*Seagulls grace the sky
above the lake from which
the Salt Lake Temple
derives its name.*